My Gratitude and Dream Journal

This journal belongs to:

Created and illustrated by Sheleen Lepar

With quotes by author Helene Pam

PURPLE SPLASH STUDIOS

Dreams and visions

help you to see

how great

YOU CAN BE.

Text copyright © 2015 by Helene Pam
Illustrations copyright © 2015 by Sheleen Lepar

All rights reserved. No parts of this book may be reproduced, transmitted, or stored in an information retrieval system in any form or by any means, graphic, electronic, or mechanical, including photocopying, taping, and recording, without prior written permission from Purple Splash Studios. For information regarding permissions, write to PurpleSplash@outlook.com.

ISBN 13: 978-0692423332
10: 0692423338

How to use this journal:

Whenever you want to capture your mood,
a moment, a dream, or your gratitude,
just choose any page, inspired by the art,
to paste pictures, draw, or write from your heart.

This book will remain a wide open door
to all that you've dreamed
and are grateful for.

Life holds special

MAGIC

for those who dare

to dream.

(Anon)

My Dreams

I'm thankful for

Build bridges of respect & acceptance...

...so relationships can bloom.

I'm grateful for

You have the ability to leave
your imprint ·················· ★*

...on the world.

Fill your
life with
color and light.

I'm thankful for

I'm grateful for

Sometimes you need to be still so that you can hear your feelings.

Every day is a new beginning.

I'm grateful for

If you never chase **YOUR DREAMS** you will never catch them.

(Anon)

My Dreams

i'm thankful for

Cherish each timeless moment.

I'm thankful for

Appreciate the little things.

I'm grateful for

The value of a true friend can never be measured.

I'm thankful for

Each of us has the key to unlock our own destiny.

I'm grateful for

Let your inner light **sparkle**

With dreams and goals,

the magic of life unfolds.

My Dreams

I'm thankful for

Be Brave. Be You.

(Anon)

Prickly situations will
strengthen who you are.

I'm thankful for

I'm grateful for

Life is full of hidden beauty.

If you look through the right lens you will see it.

I'm thankful for

Surround yourself with friends who...

...INSPIRE AND STAND BY YOU.

I'm grateful for

Everyone is born with their own special gift.

Dream big,

Aim high,

You can Learn to fly.

My Dreams

I'm grateful for

Splash, giggle, and dance in the rain.

I'm thankful for

After rough seas come calm waters.

Make time to
laugh and play.

Try to do this every day.

I'm grateful for

Let your imagination inspire you.

I'm grateful for

I'm thankful for

A butterfly is a reminder...

...that life is delicate and beautiful.

A dream will remain a

DREAM

until you take the
steps to make it a

REALITY.